5th International Joint Conference on Natural Language Processing 2011 (IJCNLP 2011)

System Demonstrations

Chiang Mai, Thailand
8 – 13 November 2011

ISBN: 978-1-62276-506-5

Printed from e-media with permission by:

Curran Associates, Inc.
57 Morehouse Lane
Red Hook, NY 12571

CURRAN ASSOCIATES INC. proceedings.com

Some format issues inherent in the e-media version may also appear in this print version.

Printed by Curran Associates, Inc. (2012)

For permission requests, please contact the Association for Computational Linguistics at the address below.

Association for Computational Linguistics
209 N. Eighth Street
Stroudsburg, Pennsylvania 18360

Phone: 1-570-476-8006
Fax: 1-570-476-0860

acl@aclweb.org

Additional copies of this publication are available from:

Curran Associates, Inc.
57 Morehouse Lane
Red Hook, NY 12571 USA
Phone: 845-758-0400
Fax: 845-758-2634
Email: curran@proceedings.com
Web: www.proceedings.com

We wish to thank our sponsors

Gold Sponsors

www.google.com

www.baidu.com

The Office of Naval Research (ONR)

The Asian Office of Aerospace Research and Development (AOARD)

Department of Systems Engineering and Engineering Managment, The Chinese University of Hong Kong

Silver Sponsors

Microsoft Corporation

Bronze Sponsors

Chinese and Oriental Languages Information Processing Society (COLIPS)

Supporter

Thailand Convention and Exhibition Bureau (TCEB)

We wish to thank our sponsors

Organizers

Asian Federation of Natural Language Processing (AFNLP)

National Electronics and Computer Technology Center (NECTEC), Thailand

Sirindhorn International Institute of Technology (SIIT), Thailand

Rajamangala University of Technology Lanna (RMUTL), Thailand

Maejo University, Thailand

Chiang Mai University (CMU), Thailand

Preface

Welcome to the proceedings of the system demonstration session. This volume contains the papers of the system demonstrations presented at the 5th International Joint Conference on Natural Language Processing, held in Chiang Mai, Thailand, on November 8, 2011.

The system demonstrations program offers the presentation of early research prototypes as well as interesting mature systems. The system demonstration chair and the members of the program committee received 5 submissions, 3 of which were selected for inclusion in the program after review by three members of the program committee.

I would like to thank the members of the program committee for their excellent job in reviewing the submissions and providing their support for the final decision.

Demonstration Co-Chairs
Kenneth Church (John Hopkins University, USA)
Yunqing Xia (Tsinghua University, China)

November 9, 2011
Chiang Mai, Thailand

Co-chairs:

Kenneth Church, John Hopkins University, USA
Yunqing Xia, Tsinghua University, China

Program Committee:

Richard Sproat, Oregon Health & Science University, USA
Qiaozhu Mei, University of Michigan, USA
Min Zhang, I2R, Singapore
Weifeng SU, United International College, China

Table of Contents

Conference Program

Wednesday, November 9, 2011

18:00–21:00 *WikiNetTK – A Tool Kit for EmbeddingWorld Knowledge in NLP Applications*
Alex Judea, Vivi Nastase and Michael Strube

18:00–21:00 *Using Linguist's Assistant for Language Description and Translation*
Stephen Beale

18:00–21:00 *TTC TermSuite - A UIMA Application for Multilingual Terminology Extraction from Comparable Corpora*
Jérôme Rocheteau and Béatrice Daille

WikiNetTK – A Tool Kit for Embedding World Knowledge in NLP Applications

Alex Judea, Vivi Nastase, Michael Strube
Heidelberg Institute for Theoretical Studies gGmbH
Heidelberg, Germany
{alexander.judea, vivi.nastase, michael.strube}@h-its.org

Abstract

WikiNetTK is a Java-based open-source toolkit for facilitating the interaction with and the embedding of world knowledge in NLP applications. For user interaction we provide a visualization component, consisting of graphical and textual browsing tools. This allows the user to inspect the knowledge base to which WikiNetTK is applied. The application-oriented part of the toolkit provides various functionalities: access to various types of information in the knowledge base as well as methods for computing association paths and relatedness measures. The system is applied to a large-scale multilingual concept network obtained by extracting and combining various sources of information from Wikipedia.

1 Introduction

Since the early 1990s the quest for large scale machine-readable knowledge repositories has become more and more intense. Cyc (Lenat and Guha, 1990) relies on experts to add to its knowledge base, MindPixel and Open Mind Common Sense (Singh, 2002) opened the contributors base to everyone using the Internet as a collaborative platform. Research in the 2000s has focused much on Wikipedia and extracting the knowledge it provides for human consumption into machine readable format. DBpedia (Auer et al., 2007) and YAGO (Suchanek et al., 2007) are two such examples. With the extraction of very large knowledge repositories it becomes crucial to provide tools for the user that would allow her to explore and use the information contained therein.

We introduce WikiNetTK (WNTK), a tool for visualizing and exploiting world knowledge extracted from Wikipedia. It is composed of three main parts: (i) an API that serves as an interface to the knowledge base used; it is currently applied to WikiNet, a concept network extracted from Wikipedia (with minor modifications this can be adapted for other, similar, knowledge bases); (ii) a visualization component, that allows the user to inspect the knowledge encoded in the resource; (iii) functionalities for computing association paths between concepts and computing semantic relatedness. WNTK also provides a command line interpreter for users who wish to work outside the Java environment; the commands implemented so far allow the user to retrieve and output concepts, paths between concepts, access the relatedness metrics and use the visualization component to directly visualize concepts or paths.

WikiNetTK[1] is an open-source Java-based system. For data management it uses BerkeleyDB[2] and for visualization prefuse[3].

2 Data

WikiNetTK is applied to WikiNet, a repository of world knowledge extracted from Wikipedia (Nastase et al., 2010). It is derived from the category and article network, disambiguation, redirect, cross-language, infobox and textual content of Wikipedia pages. It is organized as a concept network – it separates concepts and their lexicalizations, and contains relations between concepts – in a manner similar to WordNet. Concepts have lexicalizations in numerous languages. With WikiNet's 3.7 Million concepts and 40 Million relations (instantiating 656 relation types), efficiency in data management becomes an issue. Manual analysis of the data is also problematic. WikiNetTK addresses both these issues. A fast data management is the basis for the user's computations and for an easy-to-use visualization component.

[1] `http://sourceforge.net/projects/wikinettk/`

[2] `http://oracle.com/technetwork/database/berkeleydb`

[3] `http://prefuse.org`

3 System components

3.1 API

The API provides the interface between database management and data usage. This separation allows a user to easily customize the database management system (DBMS) to her needs, without an impact on the functionality of the system, as well as change the knowledge base used. WNTK's database mainly contains the following Java objects, reflecting the organization of knowledge:

1. *Concept*. A *Concept* contains a flag indicating if it denotes a named entity, the number of hyponyms it has in the network, its network depth, a definition (the first sentence in the respective Wikipedia article), a set of semantic relations to other concepts, a set of names in different languages, and a unique ID.

2. *RelationType*. Each relation type in the database is substituted with a unique ID. This has the advantage of reducing memory usage and allows for a relation to have various names, the same as for concepts. A *RelationType* provides the name of a relation type (e.g. "IS_A"), along with its frequency.

In the interaction with the database, an ID will be resolved to its corresponding concept, a term (e.g. "book") will be resolved to a set of possible concepts, a concept can be expanded with its related concepts up to a maximum distance, and we can obtain paths between concepts in the network.

To avoid re-doing expensive computations and excessive database accesses, the API provides an extra cache for computed paths and expanded concepts (represented as vectors).

Every functionality of WNTK (e.g. the visualization component) expects an abstract type of the API – which means that the user has to reimplement only a few basic I/O related methods to be able to exchange the entire database management or the data used. The actual WNTK distribution comes with Berkeley DB Java Edition, a fast, cache-based DBMS.

3.2 Visualization

When presented with a large scale machine readable repository of knowledge, manual inspection is desirable, but problematic. WNTK's visualization component is an intuitive and efficient way to examine the underlying network, in our case, WikiNet. The user can choose between a graphical network visualization, a text-based concept and path browser, which we present in Figure 1.

The user can type a term (e.g. "book"), and then choose from a set of possible concepts. Words are ambiguous. In WikiNet, in particular, concept names come from different sources: *canonical names* come from Wikipedia article titles, *aliases* come from the redirect, disambiguation pages and cross-language links. To help the selection of the concept to be visualized, the definition is shown as a tool tip when the cursor hovers above the respective list item. Once a concept is chosen it is displayed according to the visualization style, and the user can continue the exploration by clicking on the relation clusters (in the graphical version) or on the hyperlinks (in the text version).

3.2.1 Graphical Visualization

The selected concept is rendered as a node in the middle of the canvas, surrounded by its relation types. The caption of a relation type node is its respective name and the number of relations its concept has to other concepts with this particular type. For example, if a concept has seven "IS_A" relations to other concepts, the caption of the node will be "IS_A: 7". This kind of aggregation keeps the amount of rendered nodes as low as possible. The user can select which relation type node to expand, and thus explore only the parts she is interested in, leaving the rest aggregated.

Although the rendering system[4] tries to avoid overlapping edges and nodes by re-arranging them, the number of rendered elements can become very high and confusing. Parts of the displayed network can be highlighted by hovering with the cursor over concept or relation type nodes – all the nodes they are directly connected to will change color. An example is presented in the first two screenshots in Figure 1.

3.2.2 Text-based browsing

The text-based browser works with a hyperlink structure, as shown in Figure 1. The upper part of the browser field displays the number of hyponyms, named entity information, the definition, and all names. The list of names is collapsed by default and can be shown if needed. The lower part contains the concept's relations, grouped by its relation types. Every hyperlink can be explored. A history keeps track of the exploration. The text-

[4] *prefuse* is used to render the nodes and edges and to rearrange the nodes.

based browser is a good way to explore many concepts or relations in short order.

3.2.3 Text-based path browsing

In the text-based path browser the user can choose two concepts and a maximum path length. All paths between the selected concepts are then computed and displayed. If the selected concepts are both children of a concept (i.e. a common subsumer), this concept will be displayed in bold face. When the user clicks a hyperlink, the respective concept is shown in the text-based browser. The last screenshot in Figure 1 shows the usage of the path browser.

3.3 Functionalities

The API provides fast access to the knowledge base, including retrieving concepts (through their ID or lexicalizations) and their relations. Apart from these basic operations, WNTK provides methods for retrieving paths between concepts, and compute similarity, which are basic tasks for which lexical/knowledge sources are used in NLP. At this point, the toolkit contains several implementations of semantic relatedness measures, in particular Jiang and Conrath (1997), Lin (1998) and Resnik (1995) which were shown to have highest correlation with human judges on WordNet (Budanitsky and Hirst, 2006) as well as several customized measures. The user can also retrieve association paths between concepts. The set of methods can be extended by the user, and other functionalities can be added as well. We are currently working on integrating a module for text annotation relative to the embedded resource.

4 Command line tool

Our purpose was to provide a tool that facilitates the integration of world knowledge in NLP applications. For the users who do not wish to edit or interact directly with the Java source code, WNTK provides a command line interpreter constituting an intermediary layer between using the visualization component and using the API programatically. Because of increased load time of the database, the API is initialized once. After that, the user can access the information in the knowledge base through the available commands:

1. *gc*. A command to retrieve and output concept and relations information in different ways. The command handles concept IDs and terms of various length in the same way.

2. *visual*. A command to start the visualization component. It can be provided with none, one or two arguments, causing the visualization component to be initialized in different states (starting state, concept visualization, and path visualization).

3. *rel*. A command to compute semantic relatedness between any pair of terms or concept IDs, using any of the implemented relatedness measures.

Each command has a manual page, which can be accessed using *man*.

Acknowledgements

This work has been partially supported by the EC-funded project CoSyne (FP7-ICT-4-24853) and by the Klaus Tschira Foundation.

References

Sören Auer, Christian Bizer, Jens Lehmann, Georgi Kobilarov, Richard Cyganiak, and Zachary Ives. 2007. DBpedia: A nucleus for a Web of open data. In *Proceedings of the 6th International Semantic Web Conference and 2nd Asian Semantic Web Conference,* Busan, Korea, November 11-15, 2007, pages 722–735.

Alexander Budanitsky and Graeme Hirst. 2006. Evaluating WordNet-based measures of semantic distance. *Computational Linguistics*, 32(1):13–47.

Jay J. Jiang and David W. Conrath. 1997. Semantic similarity based on corpus statistics and lexical taxonomy. In *Proceedings of the 10th International Conference on Research in Computational Linguistics (ROCLING).*

Douglas B. Lenat and R. V. Guha. 1990. *Building Large Knowledge-Based Systems: Representation and Inference in the CYC Project.* Addison-Wesley, Reading, Mass.

Dekang Lin. 1998. An information-theoretic definition of similarity. In *Proceedings of the 15th International Conference on Machine Learning,* Madison, Wisc., 24–27 July 1998, pages 296–304.

Vivi Nastase, Michael Strube, Căcilia Zirn, Benjamin Boerschinger, and Anas Eghafari. 2010. WikiNet: A very large-scale multi-linguale concept network. In *Proceedings of the International Conference on Language Resources and Evaluation* Malta, 19-21 May 2010, page to appear.

Philip Resnik. 1995. Using information content to evaluate semantic similarity in a taxonomy. In *Proceedings of the 14th International Joint Conference on Artificial Intelligence,* Montréal, Canada, 20–25 August 1995, volume 1, pages 448–453.

Push Singh. 2002. The Open Mind Common Sense project.

Fabian M. Suchanek, Gjergji Kasneci, and Gerhard Weikum. 2007. YAGO: A core of semantic knowledge unifying WordNet and Wikipedia. In *Proceedings of the 16th World Wide Web Conference,* Banff, Canada, 8–12 May, 2007, pages 697–706.

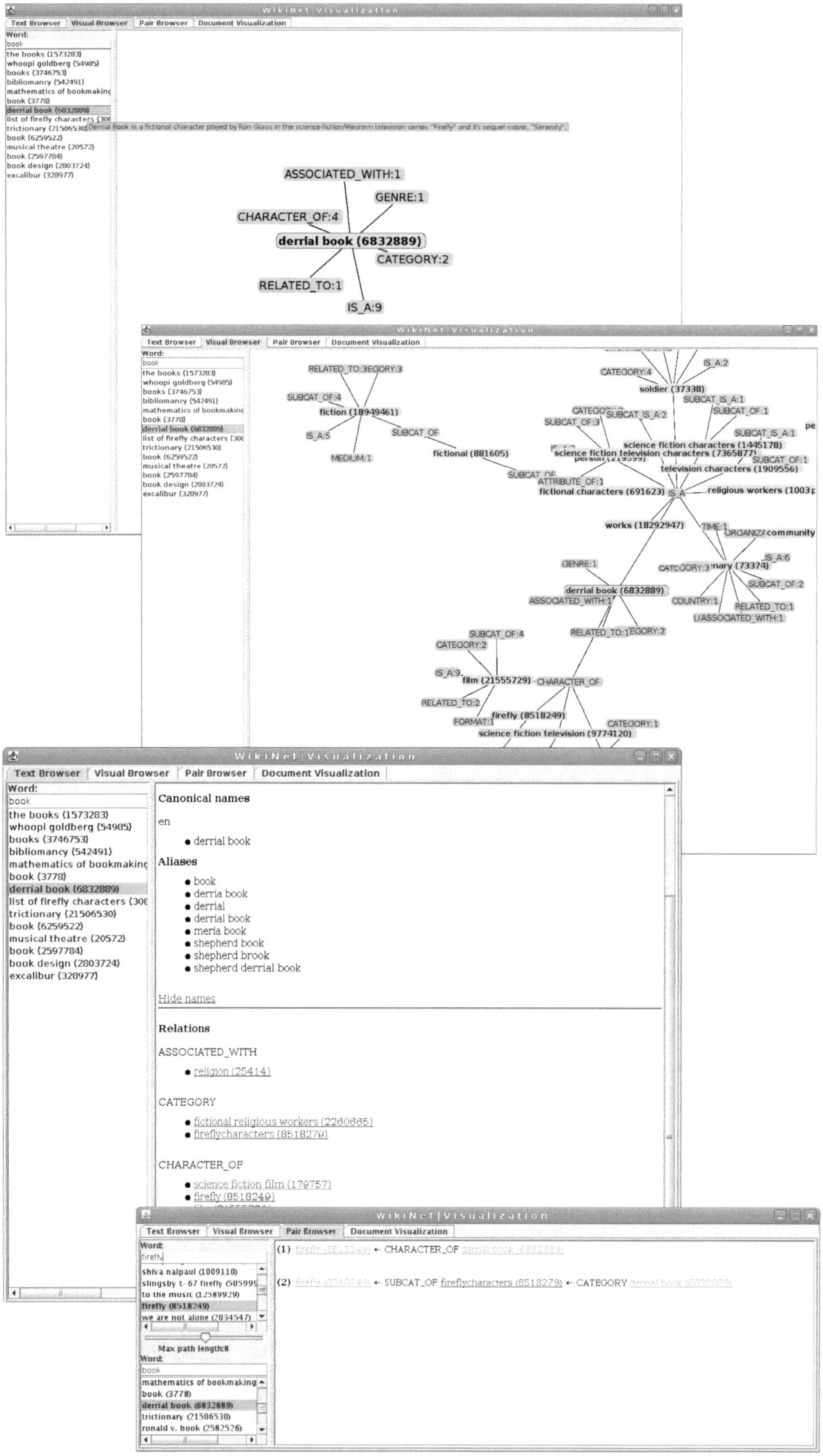

Figure 1: Graph-based, text and path visualization

Using Linguist's Assistant for Language Description and Translation

Stephen Beale
University of Maryland, Baltimore County
Baltimore, MD
sbeale@cs.umbc.edu

Abstract

The Linguist's Assistant (LA) is a practical computational paradigm for describing languages. LA seeks to specify in semantic representations a large subset of possible written communication. These semantic representations then become the starting point and organizing principle from which a linguist describes the linguistic surface forms of a language using LA's visual lexicon and grammatical rule development interface. The resulting computational description can then be used in our document authoring and translation applications.

1 Introduction

The Linguist's Assistant (LA) is a practical computational paradigm for describing languages. LA approaches the complex task of language description from two directions. From one side, LA is built on a comprehensive semantic foundation. We combine a conceptual, ontological framework with detailed semantic features that cover (or is a beginning towards the goal of covering) the range of human communication. An elicitation procedure has been built up around this central, semantic core that systematically guides the linguist through the language description process, during which the linguist builds a grammar and lexicon that "describes" how to generate target language text from the semantic representations of the elicitation corpus. The result is a "how to" guide for the language: how does one encode a given semantic representation in the language?

Coming at the problem from the other side, LA also allows the linguist to collect language data in a more conventional manner – from naturally occurring texts and linguistically motivated elicitations (for example, a linguist in Vanuatu might want to explore alienable vs. inalienable possession or serial verb constructions using naturally occurring texts). Such texts are semantically analyzed using a convenient semi-automatic document authoring interface ("authored" in our context means that a semantic representation has been prepared), in effect adding them to the standard elicitation corpus. Existing grammar rules and lexical information can then either be confirmed or adjusted, or new descriptive knowledge added that allows the built-in text generator to produce target text that is substantially equivalent to the elicited examples. The result is a "how did" guide for the language: how did a native speaker encode natural text or linguistically focused elicitations?

We believe that the combination of semantically motivated and linguistically motivated elicitation and description provides an ideal balance. The semantic-based elicitation is general and uniform across languages. It provides an efficient and relatively comprehensive standard for describing the majority of the linguistic phenomena in a language. We have found it to be an invaluable starting point in the description process. It is, however, impossible to produce a general semantic-based elicitation scheme that is not overly burdensome on the user. In addition, linguists typically know the "interesting," atypical or difficult aspects of a language. This is where linguistically based elicitation is invaluable.

A third approach to language description is encouraged in the LA framework: acquiring knowledge (lexicon and grammar) to cover preauthored texts. The semantically and linguistically motivated elicitations from the first two approaches above provide a solid foundation for lexicon and grammar development, but we have found that adding to that the experience and discipline of acquiring the knowledge necessary to generate actual texts is invaluable. This is usually

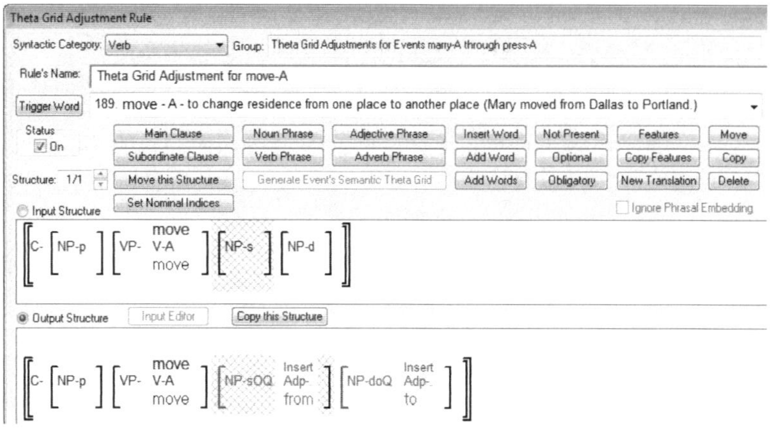

Figure 1. Visual Interface for grammatical rules

the best opportunity for documenting phenomena that are more lexically dependent since the vocabulary in the semantic-based elicitation stage is quite limited. For this reason we include several pre-authored (i.e. semantically analyzed and ready for use in our translation module) community development texts with LA.

Underlying all these approaches to knowledge acquisition in LA is a visual, semi-automatic interface for recording grammatical rules and lexical information. Figure 1 shows an example of one kind of visual interface used for "theta-grid adjustment rules." The figure shows an English rule used to adjust the "theta grid" or "case frame" of an English verb. Grammatical rules typically describe how a given semantic structure is realized in the language. The whole gamut of linguistic phenomena is covered, from morphological alternations (Figure 2) to case frame specifications to phrase structure ordering (Figure 3) to lexical collocations – and many others. These grammatical rules interplay with a rich lexical description interface that allows for assignment of word-level features and the description of lexical forms associated with individual roots (Figure 4). Currently, the linguist is responsible for the creation of rules, albeit with a natural, visual interface that often is able to set up the requisite input semantic structures automatically. We continue work on a module that will allow the semi-automatic generation of rules similar to research in the BOAS (McShane, et al., 2002), LinGO (Bender, at al., 2010), PAWS (Black and Black, 2009) and Avenue (Probst, et al., 2003) projects. Such a module will, we believe, make LA accessible to a larger pool of linguists. We also provide a growing list of rule templates that linguists can use to describe common linguistic phenomena.

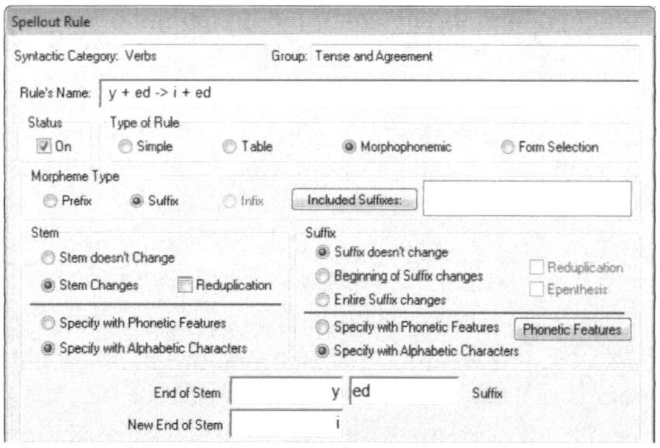

Figure 2. Morphological alternation rule

Integrated with these elicitation and description tools is a text generator that allows for immediate confirmation of the validity of grammatical rules and lexical information. We also provide an interface for tracking the scope and examples of grammatical rules. This minimizes the possibility of conflicting or duplicate rules while providing the linguist a convenient index into the work already accomplished. And finally, we provide a utility for producing a written description of the language - after all, a computational description of a language is of no practical use (outside of translation applications) unless it can be conveniently referenced. Refer to Beale (submitted) for a comprehensive description of Linguist's Assistant.

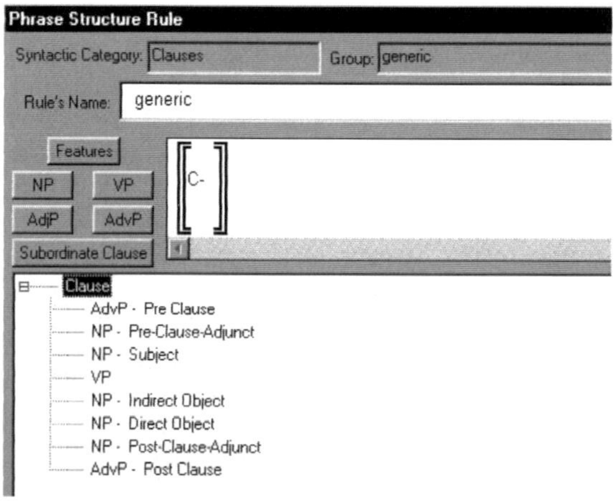

Figure 3. Phrase structure ordering rule

	Stems	Glosses	infinitive	present indic 1st sing
1	aprend	learn	aprender	aprendo
2	habl	speak	hablar	hablo
3	ten	have	tener	tengo
4	viv	live	vivir	vivo

present indic 2nd sing	present indic 3rd sing	present indic 1st pl	present indic 3rd pl
aprendes	aprende	aprendemos	aprenden
hablas	habla	hablamos	hablan
tienes	tiene	tenemos	tienen
vives	vive	vivimos	viven

Figure 4. Lexical forms for Spanish

LA has been used to produce extensive grammars and lexicons for Jula (a Niger-Congo language), Kewa (Papua New Guinea), North Tanna (Vanuatu), Korean and English. Work continues in two languages of Vanuatu, with additional languages planned in the near future. The resulting computational resources have been used in our separate document authoring and translation applications to produce a significant amount of high-quality translations in each of these languages. Figures 5 and 6 present translations of a section of a medical text on AIDS into English Korean. Please reference Beale et al. (2005) and Allman and Beale (2004; 2006) for more information on using LA in translation projects, and for documentation on the evaluations of the translations produced. Note: LA can be used as the language-description module within our larger applications called TA (The Translator's Assistant, for translating health and community development materials, as well as "authoring" new texts) or TBTA (The Bible Translator's Assistant, for those interested in Bible Translation). We argue that the high quality results achieved in translation projects demonstrate the quality and coverage of the underlying language description that LA produces.

Kande's Story 1:1 Title: Kande's mother knows a secret.

Kande's Story 1:2 One day a girl named Kande was sitting near a tree. Kande was reading a book. She had a younger sister named Teshi. Teshi ran to Kande. Teshi was very excited. She said to Kande, "Kande! Kande! I heard certain women talking to each other. Those women said that mother knows a secret! Do you know mother's secret?"

Kande's Story 1:3 Kande said, "I might know mother's secret. We should go to our house and talk to our mother. Mother might tell us about her secret. I'll race you to our house!"

Kande's Story 1:4 Kande and Teshi ran to their house quickly. When Kande and Teshi arrived at the house, they were laughing. They had two younger sisters. One younger sister's name was Falala. And the other younger sister's name was Iniko. Kande and Teshi also had a younger brother named Jumoke. Falala, Iniko, and Jumoke heard Kande and Teshi laughing. So they ran to the door to see Kande and Teshi. Then mother said to all the children, "Be quiet because your father has to sleep." Then she walked from

Figure 5. English translation of a medical text

Korean

Kande's Story 1:1 제목: 칸디의 어머니는 비밀을 알고 있어요.

Kande's Story 1:2 어느 날 칸디라는 소녀가 나무 가까이에 앉아 있었다. 칸디는 책을 읽고 있었다. 칸디는 태쉬라는 여동생이 있었다. 태쉬는 칸디에게 달려갔다. 태쉬는 매우 흥분하였다. 태쉬는 칸디에게 말하였다. "언니! 언니! 나는 어떤 여자들이 서로에게 말하는 것을 들었어요. 이 여자들은 어머니께서 비밀을 알고 계시다고 말하였어요! 언니는 어머니의 비밀을 알고 있어요?"

Figure 6. Korean translation of a medical text

2 Content of the Demonstration

A partial example of the content of the proposed demonstration can be found at http://ilit.umbc.edu/sbeale/LA/ under the "Demo Videos" link. These demonstration videos are part of an online journal article (Beale, submitted) that describes LA in depth. A draft of this journal article can be found at the same website under the "Publications" link.

We will be prepared to demonstrate, as appropriate to the interests of a particular group of participants, the following:

- An overview of LA
- The semantic representation system
- The document authoring system that enables the semi-automatic analysis of new texts or elicitations
- How to create lexicons that are appropriate for different kinds of languages
- How to use the visual rule creation interface to create various kinds of grammatical rules
- Multilingual examples of lexicons
- Multilingual examples of grammatical rules
- Multilingual examples of translation results

We will also prepare 10 minute modules with "hands-on" examples for any interested participants who wish to take a bit more time investigating LA.

3 Previous Experience in Teaching LA

LA is the basis of a semester-long Honor's College class at the University of Maryland, Baltimore County. In that class we present an overview of different types of linguistic phenomena. We then use LA to encode descriptive knowledge of multi-lingual examples of each. The class size is 25 students.

We have also prepared tutorials and online demonstrations (http://ilit.umbc.edu/sbeale/LA/) and informally used LA with a number of field linguists.

4 Required Resources

We require a single projector. Internet service is not necessary.

5 Acknowledgements

The author gratefully acknowledges the partnership of Tod Allman from the University of Texas, Arlington. Dr. Allman is co-developer of LA.

References

Allman, Tod. 2010. The translator's assistant: a multilingual natural language generator based on linguistic universals, typologies, and primitives. Arlington, TX: University of Texas dissertation.

Tod Allman and Stephen Beale. 2006. "A natural language generator for minority languages," in Proceedings of SALTMIL, Genoa, Italy.

Tod Allman and Stephen Beale. 2004. "An environment for quick ramp-up multi-lingual authoring," International Journal of Translation 16(1).

Stephen Beale. Submitted. "Documenting endangered languages with linguist's assistant." Language Documentation and Conservation Journal. Draft available at: http://ilit.umbc.edu/sbeale/LA/papers/DEL-for-LDC-journal.pdf

Stephen Beale, S. Nirenburg, M. McShane, and Tod Allman. 2005. "Document authoring the Bible for minority language translation," in Proceedings of MT-Summit, Phuket, Thailand.

Emily Bender, S. Drellishak, A. Fokkens, M. Goodman, D. Mills, L. Poulson, and S. Saleem. 2010. "Grammar prototyping and testing with the LinGO grammar matrix customization system," in Proceedings of the ACL 2010 System Demonstrations.

Sheryl Black and Andrew Black. 2009. "PAWS: parser and writer for syntax: drafting syntactic grammars in the third wave," http://www.sil.org/silepubs/PUBS/51432/SILForum2009-002.pdf.

Marjorie McShane, Sergei Nirenburg, Jim Cowie, and Ron Zacharski. 2002. "Embedding knowledge elicitation and MT systems within a single architecture," Machine Translation 17(4), pp.271-305.

Katharina Probst, Lori Levin, Erik Petersen, Alon Lavie and Jaime Carbonell. 2003. "MT for minority languages using elicitation-based learning of syntactic transfer rules," Machine Translation 17(4), pp.245-270.

TTC TermSuite
A UIMA Application for Multilingual Terminology Extraction from Comparable Corpora

Jérôme Rocheteau **Béatrice Daille**
University of Nantes - LINA
2, rue de la Houssinière
BP 92208 – F-44322 Nantes cedex 3
{jerome.rocheteau,beatrice.daille}@univ-nantes.fr

Abstract

This paper aims at presenting TTC TermSuite: a tool suite for multilingual terminology extraction from comparable corpora. This tool suite offers a user-friendly graphical interface for designing UIMA-based tool chains whose components (i) form a functional architecture, (ii) manage 7 languages of 5 different families, (iii) support standardized file formats, (iv) extract single- and multi- word terms languages by languages (v) and align them by pairs of languages.

1 Introduction

Lexicons and terminologies play a central role in any machine translation tool, regardless of the theoretical foundations upon which the machine translation (MT) tool is based (e.g. statistical machine translation or rule-based machine translation, example-based translation, etc.). Terminologies may be extracted from parallel corpora, i.e. from previously translated texts, but such corpora are scarce. Previously translated data is still sparse and only available for some pairs of languages and few specific domains, such as Europarl (Koehn, 2005). Thus, no parallel corpora are available for most specialized domains, especially for emerging domains. Several tool suites exist for multilingual term extraction for parallel corpora: the GIZA++ statistical machine translation toolkit (Och and Ney, 2003), the iTools suite that performs single- and multi- word alignment, and includes graphical and interactive tools (Merkel and Foo, 2007). To tackle the drawbacks of term alignment from parallel corpora, comparable corpora that are "sets of texts in different languages that are not translations of each other" (Bowker and Pearson, 2002, p. 93) seem to be the right solution to solve textual scarcity. The bilingual alignment is performed thanks to contextual analysis such as (Rapp, 1995). TTC TermSuite is the first tool suite for the multilingual extraction of terminology from comparable corpora. It is multilingually designed, adopting a 4-step functional architecture and using the UIMA open solution.

TTC TermSuite is designed to perform bilingual term extraction from comparable corpora in five European languages: English, French, German, Spanish and one under-resourced language, Latvian, as well as in Chinese and Russian. TTC TermSuite is a 4-step functional architecture that is driven by the required inputs and provided outputs of each tool. The bilingual term alignment (step 4) requires processes of monolingual term extraction (step 3), itself requiring preliminary linguistic analysis (step 2) that requires text processing (step 1). TTC TermSuite is based on the UIMA framework which supports applications that analyze large volumes of unstructured information. UIMA was developed initially by IBM (Ferrucci and Lally, 2004) but is now an Apache project[1]. UIMA enables such applications to be decomposed into components (and components into sub-components) and to aggregate the latter easily. TTC TermSuite includes a graphical user interface tool with several embedded UIMA components that perform text and linguistic analysis up to monolingual term extraction and bilingual term alignment.

First, we present TTC TermSuite specifications that include the 4-step functional architecture in reverse order, the data model, and the input and output formats. Then, we detail the UIMA-based implementation, its components, the multilingualism management and the graphical interface for building tool chains easily. We conclude by the case study: the extraction of SWTs from a comparable corpora in two pairs of languages.

[1] http://uima.apache.org

Functional Architecture	Required/Input data	Provided/Output data
Text Pre-Processing		text, language
Linguistic Analysis	text, language	word, part-of-speech lemma
word tokenization	text, language	word
part-of-speech tagging	language, word	part-of-speech
lemmatization	language, word, part-of-speech	lemma
Term Extraction	language, word, part-of-speech lemma	term
Term Alignment	language, term	binary relation over terms

Table 1: TTC TermSuite 4-step Functional Architecture & Data Model

2 Specifications

The TTC TermSuite specifications consist of the definition of functional computing units within an architecture, the data model shared between these units and the file formats of this data model. Table 1 summarizes the 4-step functional architecture, and the input and output data types for each functional step.

2.1 Functional Architecture

The functional architecture is divided into 4 steps: text pre-processing, linguistic analysis, monolingual term extraction, bilingual term alignment. A set of tools will be assigned to each step:

Text pre-processing web-crawlers, text categorizers, text extractors, data cleaning, language recognizers, etc. All tools that provide a clean textual content without any linguistic information.

Linguistic analysis word tokenizers, part-of-speech taggers, lemmatizers, morphological analyzers and syntactic parsers.

Term extraction single-word term (SWT), multi-word term (MWT) and morphological compound detection, term variant processing such as acronym detection;

Term alignment SWT and MWT alignment, cognate detection, machine translation on the fly for MWTs.

2.2 Data Model

The TTC TermSuite's 4-step architecture requires a data model that defines the data types required as input and output for each functional unit. The output of the *text pre-processing* step should provide at a minimum the textual data of the document and the language it is written in. Textual data and language are required by the *linguistic analysis* step. According to the language, miscellaneous treatments are applied to the textual data that could be useful for the *term extraction* step such as part-of-speech and lemma taggers, morphological analysis. Part-of-speech and lemma are required for the *term extraction* step that performs both SWT and MWT extraction. The output of the *term extraction* step is a list of candidate terms that is required by the *term alignment* step. TTC TermSuite outputs one-to-many alignments: a source term associated to the set of its most probable target translations in the target language. It should be noticed that the first two steps deal with the document processing whereas the last two steps deal with the document collection processing.

2.3 Input and Output Formats

TTC TermSuite's input and output files are XML files which adopts standard formats. Document features are formatted according to the Dublin Core XML Schema. A Dublin Core input file with the location, the language, the format of the resource can be represented as follows:

```
<metadata>
  <language>english</language>
  <format>text/html</format>
  <title>Top Myths About Wind Energy</title>
  <source>
    http://www.bwea.com/energy/myths.html
  </source>
  <subject>
    wind energy, wind turbine, wind farm, wind power plant
  </subject>
</metadata>
```

Moreover, the terms that have led to *crawl* this document is also provided by the Dublin Core subject element.

As for terminologies, they are formatted according to the TermBase eXchange XML Schema (TBX) [ISO 30042:2008] compliant with the TMF (Terminological Markup Framework) meta-model [ISO 16642:2001]. Such an output file with an alignment between English and Chinese for the term *wind energy* corresponds to the sample below:

```
<martif type="TBX">
  <text>
    <body>
      <termEntry id="term-entry-1">
        <langSet xml:lang="en">
          <tig>
            <term id="term-1">wind energy</term>
            <descrip type="alignment" target="term-16"/>
          </tig>
        </langSet>
      </termEntry>
      <termEntry id="term-entry-16">
        <langSet xml:lang="zh">
          <tig>
            <term id="term-16">风能</term>
            <descrip type="alignment" target="term-1"/>
          </tig>
        </langSet>
      </termEntry>
    </body>
  </text>
</martif>
```

Terms and term entries of the TermBase eXchange files provided by the TTC TermSuite can be enriched with other features such as the term constituent, their part-of-speech, their lemma, their different occurrences in the corpora, etc according to the linguistic analyzes that have been processed.

3 UIMA implementation

The UIMA-based implementation consists of components that can be easily aggregated together through a user-friendly graphical interface, are powered by the UIMA framework, and are designed to manage multilingualism.

3.1 Graphical Interface

With the TTC TermSuite, it is possible to design UIMA tool chains easily; users can create or open several tool chains. They can select their components merely by dragging them from the available ones and dropping them on the selected ones. Component metadata can be displayed by double clicking on an available component whereas component parameters can be set by double clicking on a selected one. There are TTC TermSuite panels for processing tool chains and viewing their results such as illustrated in the Figure 1.

3.2 UIMA Components

UIMA offers a common, standards-based software architecture facilitating reuse and integration, it solves essentially issues connected with lower-level interoperability of software components. UIMA main concepts are:

Collection Processing Engine (CPE) Tool chains are formalised by CPE within UIMA. They are defined by 1 Collection Reader and by 1 or more Analysis Engine.

Common Analysis Structure (CAS) UIMA adopts a common representation to represent any artifact being analyzed and to provide reading/writing access to the analysis results or annotations. CAS ensures CPE component interoperability thanks to a **Type System** that can be indexed in CAS.

Collection Readers are the only CPE components able to create CAS.

Analysis Engines are CPE components that produce structured information by indexing annotations in CAS.

Up to now more than 60 components are provided within the TTC TermSuite but 4 of them can be drawn out that corresponds to the 4 steps of the functional architecture. The first 2 steps are completed. Step 3 and 4 are still under development but are completed for SWTs.

1. **Text Preprocessing** is a Collection Reader creates CAS from Dublin Core metadata.

2. **Linguistic Analysis** is an Analysis Engine that detects words, their part-of-speech and their lemma.

3. **Term Extraction** is an Analysis Engine that adopts a homogeneous approach for both SWTs and MWTs. Terms are first extract thanks to morpho-syntactic patterns defined for each languages and rank according to statistical criteria (Daille, 2002).

4. **Term Alignment** is an Analysis Engine that aligns SWTs using a lexical context analysis (Morin et al., 2010)

UIMA components are provided through out a Google Code repository for managing Open-Source source code[2].

[2]http://code.google.com/p/ttc-project/

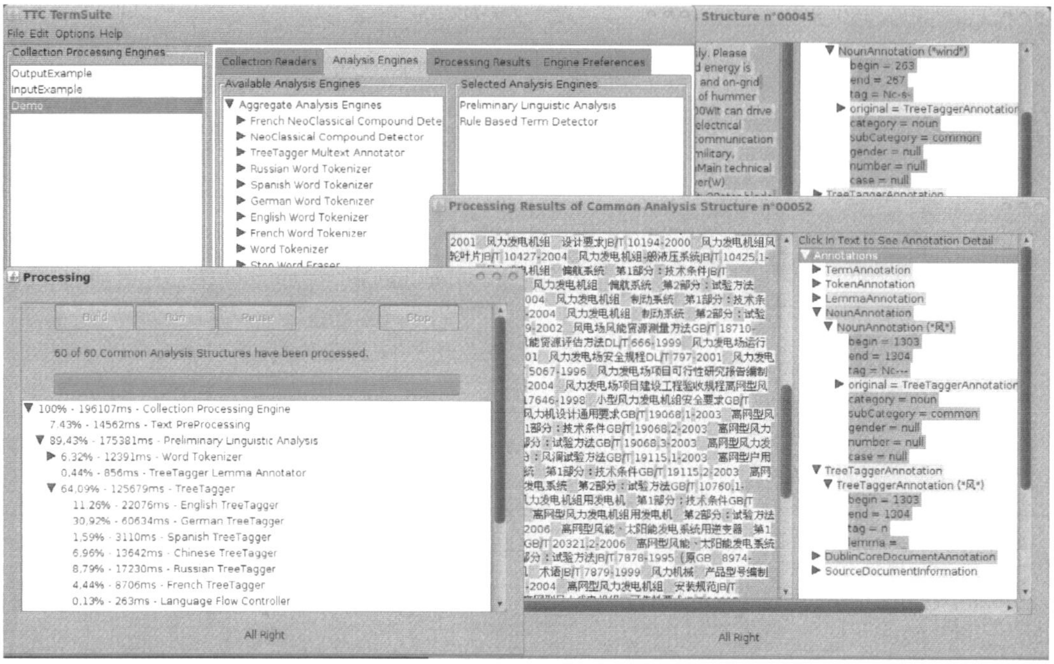

Figure 1: Graphical interface of TTC TermSuite

3.3 Multilingual Management

Multilingualism is delegated to CPE components level e.g. to Analysis Engines. As the language of the CAS is set by the Text PreProcessing Collection Reader and as each Analysis Engine specifies which languages they analyze, CAS can be dispatched to the corresponding AE.

4 Demonstration

The TTC TermSuite will be demonstrated using the following case study: it will extract SWTs from comparable corpora that deal with renewable energy for two pairs of languages: French-English and English-Chinese.

Acknowledgement

The research leading to these results has received funding from the European Communitys Seventh Framework Programme (*/*FP7/2007-2013*/*) under Grant Agreement no 248005.

References

[Bowker and Pearson2002] Lynne Bowker and Jennifer Pearson. 2002. *Working with Specialized Language: A Practical Guide to Using Corpora*. London/New York: Routledge.

[Daille2002] Béatrice Daille. 2002. Terminology mining. In Maria Teresa Pazienza, editor, *SCIE*, volume 2700 of *Lecture Notes in Computer Science*, pages 29–44. Springer.

[Ferrucci and Lally2004] David Ferrucci and Adam Lally. 2004. Uima: an architectural approach to unstructured information processing in the corporate research environment. *Natural Language Engineering*, 10:327–348, September.

[Koehn2005] Philipp Koehn. 2005. Europarl: A Parallel Corpus for Statistical Machine Translation. In *Conference Proceedings: the tenth Machine Translation Summit*, pages 79–86, Phuket, Thailand. AAMT, AAMT.

[Merkel and Foo2007] Magnus Merkel and Jody Foo. 2007. Terminology extraction and term ranking for standardizing term banks. In *Proceedings of the 16th Nordic Conference of Computational Linguistics (NODALIDA-07)*, pages 349–354, Tartu.

[Morin et al.2010] Emmanuel Morin, Béatrice Daille, Koichi Takeuchi, and Kyo Kageura. 2010. Brains, not brawn: The use of "smart" comparable corpora in bilingual terminology mining. *TSLP*, 7(1).

[Och and Ney2003] Franz Josef Och and Hermann Ney. 2003. A systematic comparison of various statistical alignment models. *Computational Linguistics*, 29(1):19–51.

[Rapp1995] Reinhard Rapp. 1995. Identify Word Translations in Non-Parallel Texts. In *Proceedings of the 35th Annual Meeting of the Association for Computational Linguistics (ACL'95)*, pages 320–322, Boston, MA, USA.

Author Index